Seven Sisters

A fascinating insight into the lives of the women of the Wesley family in the eighteenth century.

G M Best

ISBN 978-1-901084-85-6

Text copyright © The Author 2011

Printed and published by
WOODSPRING RESOURCE CENTRE
Locking, Weston-super-Mare, BS24 8BB
Tel: 01934 820800

For
THE NEW ROOM
John Wesley's Chapel, 36 The Horsefair, Bristol BS1 3JE

THE SEVEN SISTERS

John and Charles Wesley had seven gifted sisters and their lives provide a real insight into the way in which women were often appallingly treated in an era when they were expected to always obey their fathers, husbands, and brothers.

All seven sisters were initially given an unusually good start in life because they received an education way beyond what was normal for women in their day. This stemmed mainly from the work of their mother Susanna, who was one of the most well-read women of her day, but it also owed much to the way their father Samuel was happy for them to use his extensive library. However, they simultaneously faced grinding poverty in order that their father and brothers could have opportunities denied them. Bar one, they were not given the dowries that normally assisted women to acquire appropriate husbands. Their education eventually proved a curse rather than a blessing because most of the men with whom they came into contact were intellectually far inferior to them. Matters were made worse for the sisters by the often callous way in which their father and older brothers interfered in their choice of potential partners. All of them ended up in relationships with men who treated them badly.

This book shows how family poverty, broken romances, unhappy marriages and early loss of children devastated the seven sisters' lives. However, it also depicts how each of these seven women in her own way sought to rise above her circumstances, often using faith in God as a means to endure the unendurable.

1. BROKEN ROMANCES

The tragic story of Emily Wesley

Emilia or, as she was more commonly called 'Emily' or 'Em', was the first daughter of Samuel and Susanna Wesley to survive infancy. She was born on 31 December 1692 and baptized at St Leonard's Church in South Ormsby near Louth on 13 January 1693. She grew up to be not only attractive but also good-humoured, level-headed, quick-witted, and intelligent. Though educated entirely at home, she became quite a scholar through free access to her father's library. It is said she had a prodigious memory and a particularly good ear for poetry and music. John Wesley said it was a joy to hear her reading aloud the verse of John Milton.

As the eldest surviving daughter, she was especially close to her mother, not least because Susanna's frequent pregnancies forced her to rely on Emily's support in bringing up the rest of the family. Her younger sister Hetty later wrote of Emily:

> 'Virtue, form and wit, in thee
> Move in perfect harmony....
> Thy graceful form with pleasure I survey;
> It charms the eye – the heart – away....
> To all thy outward majesty and grace,
> To all the blooming features of they face;
> To all the heavenly sweetness of thy mind,
> A noble, generous, equal soul is joined,
> By reason polished, and by arts refined.'

When the Epworth Rectory was destroyed by fire in February 1709 it was the seventeen-year old Emily who alone stayed with her parents amid the chaos, whilst all the younger children were temporarily placed with friends and relatives. Being her mother's confidante made her quickly appreciate that her parents were financially ruined and so Emily accepted her lot without complaint:

'I lived easy… having most necessaries, though few diversions, and never going abroad. Yet after working all day, I read some pleasant book at night, and was contented enough.'

When Susanna chose in 1711 to write a religious treatise about God for the benefit of her younger children, she chose to write it as a conversation between her and the eminently sensible Emily and it probably did reflect the many religious discussions in which they had engaged. It was Emily who discovered the book on Danish missionaries in her father's library that encouraged Susanna to take the brave step of leading worship for parishioners when her husband was away from home. Susanna recorded the impact of Emily reading the book to her:

'At last it came into my mind, though I am not a man nor a minister of the gospel, and so cannot be employed in such a worthy employment as they were, yet if my heart were sincerely devoted to God, and if I were inspired with a true zeal for his glory and really did desire the salvation of souls, I might do somewhat more than I do.' Emily's sisters found it difficult to return to the isolation of Epworth and Hetty Wesley was later to express her amazement at how Emily was prepared to permit her 'brilliant virtues' to be immured in 'a noxious irksome den'. In fact Emily was increasingly impatient with her father's failure to resolve the family finances and his readiness to spend money on himself by engaging in expensive visits to London every winter, leaving her and the rest of the family in 'intolerable want and affliction':

'Then I learnt what it was to seek money for bread, seldom having any without such hardships in getting it that much abated the pleasure of it. Thus we went on, growing worse and worse; all of us children in scandalous want of necessaries for years together; vast income but no comfort or credit with it.'

"Lincoln, where for a number of years Emily lived"

In 1716 Emily was sent to London in the hope her uncle, Matthew Wesley, who was a wealthy physician, could find her suitable employment as a governess. She failed to obtain employment but, whilst there, she met and fell madly in love with a friend of her brother Samuel called Robert Laybourne. He was a far cry from any male she had met in isolated Epworth because he was charming in manner and very well educated, having studied at Westminster School and Christ Church College,

Oxford. He was, in Emily's words, a man of 'the highest understanding' and possessed of 'the sweetest temper in England'. Leybourne told Emily he reciprocated her love but that he was not yet financially in a position to marry her. When she returned home, they kept in regular written contact for three years:

'When anything grieved me he was my comforter; when affliction pressed hard on me he was hard at hand to relieve me; …… although our affairs grew no better, yet I was tolerable easy, thinking his love sufficient recompense for the loss or absence of all other worldly comforts.'

It was whilst she was back at home that the family experienced the famous alleged 'haunting' of Epworth by a poltergeist from Dec 1716 to January 1717. Emily was at first totally skeptical, but eventually felt compelled to accept the reality of the strange knockings and unaccountable movement of objects. In February she wrote to her eldest brother Samuel:

'I am so far from being superstitious that I was too much inclined to infidelity, so that I heartily rejoice at having such an opportunity of convincing myself, past doubt or scruple, of the existence of some beings besides those we see.'

She nicknamed the poltergeist 'Old Jeffery' after a man called Jeffrey Fletcher, who had died the previous August. Her mother also reluctantly came to accept the haunting was real, though she told her family not to speak of the matter. Historians tend to ascribe the alleged haunting to Hetty Wesley. Only Emily was ever to say that she subsequently thought she might have heard Jeffery again – and that was inexplicably many years later in 1750 in London.

In the winter of 1718 Susanna ordered Emily to desist her correspondence with Laybourne, though he had become a fellow of Brasenose College in Oxford. Emily says the ban arose because of malicious advice by a 'near relation' but equally hints that something she did contributed to her mother's action. We do not know what her 'indiscretion' (as she calls it) was. It is usually assumed that the near relation was her older brother Samuel or his wife, who either discovered something discreditable about Leybourne or thought his attentions to Emily were insincere. Her lover made no attempt as far as we know to oppose the decision to end their contact and this may explain why Emily herself put up no fight, though she was heart-broken. She vowed never to marry anyone else.

Family circumstances may also have contributed to Emily's initial acquiescence. Her mother was taken very seriously ill that winter and confined to bed whilst her father was under continual threat of being arrested for debt. Emily found herself in charge of the family. She afterwards wrote:

'That dismal winter I shall ever remember… expecting my mother's death every day and my father's confinement [in prison]; and yet in all this care the loss of Leybourne was the heaviest. For near half a year I never slept half a night."

Once Susanna was recovered, Emily resolved to leave home in the spring of 1719 and go 'into the world'. She took up a vacancy at a boarding school in Lincoln and 'fell readily into that way of life':

'I was so pleased to see myself in good clothes, with money in my pocket, and respected in a strange manner by everyone, that I seemed to have gotten into another world.'

This was her life for five years until the school unfortunately had to close in 1723. Her mother, who had sorely missed her, persuaded her to return home, saying she would find things much easier because her father had acquired a second living (that of Wroot) to add to his income as Rector of Epworth and this 'would make him a rich man in a few years'. She promised that as parents they would allow Emily 'all the liberties in their power'. Emily agreed and initially her return proved acceptable. She had the money she had saved to buy what she felt necessary and to fund a four-month stay in Lincoln when she tired of the isolation. However, once her money ran out, it was a different matter. By the winter of 1724 she was sharing once more in her family's poverty and she saw her decision to return as the product of 'an evil hour ':

'Every trifling want was either not supplied, or I had more trouble to procure it than it was worth.... Could I lay aside all thought of the future, and could I be content without three things, money, liberty, and clothes, I might live comfortably.'

It was obvious to Emily that the additional income derived from Wroot would simply go 'to pay some part of those infinite debts my father had run into' rather than making the family financially comfortable.

Emily used her return to try and get her family to reconsider her being allowed to marry Robert Leybourne. However, in April 1725 she reluctantly decided it was useless to persevere in the face of the continued family opposition, especially after she heard that her brother Samuel had engaged in a bitter argument with Laybourne. She confided her hurt to her brother John, whom she decided to treat as her confidante, although he was ten years younger:

'No more shall I write or receive letters to and from that person. But lest you should run into a mistake and think we have quarreled, like Sam and him, I assure you that we are perfect friends; we think, wish, and judge alike, but what avails it? We are both miserable. He has not differed with my mother, but she loves him not, because she esteems him the unlucky cause of a deep melancholy in a beloved child. For his own sake it is that I cease writing, because it is now his interest to forget me.'

Emily asked John not to tell anyone about the contents of her letter: 'Let me have one relation I can trust, never give any hint to anyone of aught I write to you.' But she urged him to learn from her bitter experience:

'If my advice be worth listening to, never engage your affections before your worldly affairs are in such a posture that you may marry very soon.... Were I to live my time over again... I would not wait one year. I know you are a young man, encompassed with difficulties.... but, believe me, if ever you come to suffer the torment of a hopeless love, all other afflictions will seem small in comparison of it.'

John honoured her desire for confidentiality so her parents remained unaware of Emily's decision. That summer Susanna Wesley wrote to him expressing her concerns as to whether Robert Laybourne was a suitable suitor for Emily:

'I have somewhat against that man, but I hope he is good in the main, and I think humanity and good breeding are not among his wants.'

Though she was depressed, Emily told John he must not over-worry about her because she had enough to eat and drink and clothe herself. Moreover, she knew their mother needed her:

'She is so very good to me and has so little comfort in the world besides, that I think it barbarous to abandon her.... Whatever people may say of me here, I hope to meet happiness in the other world if not in this.'

However by January 1727 Susanna believed Emily's health had declined to such an extent that they had to get her away from Epworth unless they wished to see her die. It was agreed Emily should take up another teaching post in Lincoln, this time in a school run by a Mrs. Taylor. Emily took up her new post in May and soon 'had the whole care of the school'. This enabled her to provide employment for her youngest sister Kezzy as a teacher assistant. Samuel Wesley visited his two daughters just before Christmas 1728, but Emily found this experience difficult. He still believed the family would one day be prosperous, whilst she felt her father would 'never be worth a groat' and 'we of the female part of the family be consequently left to get our bread or starve'. She told her brother John:

'He seemed very reserved to me, and I the same to him. He said nothing to me of my going home.... [but] he thought fit to speak his mind before he went out of town to a friend of his, who told his wife and.... she told me their conference; but let them think what they please, 'tis now impossible for me to move.'

Robert Leybourne still featured highly in her thoughts. In 1729 she asked John to keep up a good correspondence with 'the unhappy L' who had been made miserable by the false accusations brought against him. As for herself, she saw death as 'a consummation devoutly to be wished'.

SEVEN SISTERS

By 1730 Mrs Taylor was failing to pay Emily and Kezzy their proper salaries. Kezzy therefore returned to Epworth and, in January 1731, so too did Emily, who felt duty bound to help nurse her sister Sukey who had become dangerously ill. Fortunately her uncle Matthew Wesley now stepped in by offering to provide her with some money towards the cost of creating a school of her own in Gainsborough. In February Emily wrote to her brother John that Mrs. Taylor had accepted her resignation 'with an indifference I did not expect' and that Gainsborough offered her 'a fairer prospect… than I could hope for'. Her greatest problem was lack of sufficient funds to properly set up the school so she faced borrowing money. She philosophically commented that 'troubles of that kind I am used to'. She asked John to pray that she would 'bear cheerfully the ills of life' and not permit problems 'to cloud the natural cheerfulness of my temper'.

Her mother clearly did not want Emily to go – that summer she told John she was struggling because of age and infirmity to run the household and that she needed Emily's support because Molly, her remaining daughter at home, was 'a good girl but unequal to the work' because of her physical disability. Despite this, Emily could not be persuaded to return home. However, in 1733 she did come to the conclusion that Robert Leybourne had never deserved her love. That is not surprising because by then not only had he been established for three years as Rector of St Anne's, Limehouse, but also he was married to someone else! She told John:

'When I loved L. he loved not me, though he was rogue enough to persuade me he did. Well, so much for that!'

Though approaching forty, she was still attractive and she entered into a relationship with a local doctor, whom we think was called Huntingdon. She described him to John as 'a companion and friend to whom I could speak freely at all times and… a most passionate lover'. To her horror, John, whose judgement she had come to trust, insisted it was unthinkable she should marry the man because he was a Quaker. He ordered her to immediately break with him. In the tensions that resulted Emily and her lover quarreled. According to Emily it was over a couple of trivial issues – she objected to some of his political views and he was foolishly jealous of the attention she gave to one of her young gentleman boarders. The quarrel provided enough impetus for her to justify in her own mind taking John's advice and ceasing to see him. That this was a decision of the head and not the heart is evident in her resulting despair:

'But now what is there in life worth valuing? Truly not much, and if I should comply with my mother's earnest desire – throw up my business here and go home – I do not see there would be much in it, since my Creator seems to have decreed to me a state of suffering here, and always deprives me of what I love, or embitters it to me.'

Emily later felt she had allowed herself to be unduly swayed by her brother. She had made him 'my intimate companion, my counselor in difficulties, the dear partner of my joys and griefs' and he had abused that trust. One of the arguments used by John in getting her to drop her lover was that she was making the world her God by 'seeking for happiness in this life'. In hindsight Emily challenged this, saying she believed God did not 'delight in the misery of any of his creatures' and that he would not have created people 'with their several desires and tendencies' unless he intended them to love another person. She told her brother she had allowed her love for him to influence her too much and that he had, like many another clergyman, assumed 'a dominion over your fellow-servants which never was designed you by God'.

Such criticism did not deter John from again determining her behaviour. In 1735 their father died and this meant the parish of Epworth passed out of the family's control. John therefore believed it was time Emily should marry because otherwise she might end up homeless if anything happened to her work. He advised her to marry a travelling apothecary called Robert Harpur, whom the Wesley family had known for some time. He was, for example, the person who had provided medical treatment for their father Samuel and their sister Molly in 1731 and 1734 respectively. Emily agreed to do what he suggested and entered into a loveless marriage in August 1735. However, it soon became clear Harpur wanted her money more than her. He had no scruples in spending the income from her school and, in the process, soon destroyed its viability. It was not long before he had reduced her to dire poverty. To add to Emily's unhappiness their one child – a daughter called 'Tetty' – died while still young.

Emily invited her widowed mother to live with her but Susanna soon tired of the constant squabbling between husband and wife and left to take up residence with her son Samuel instead. In 1738 John did not even visit Emily on his return from missionary work in America, preferring instead to travel to Germany to visit Moravian communities. Emily was understandably angry at the way she had been abandoned. When he wrote to her of his exciting experiences, she replied:

'For God's sake, tell me how a distressed woman, who expects daily to have the very bed taken from under her for rent, can consider the state of the churches in Germany. I am ready to give up the ghost with grief…. We owe at Christmas two years rent … I have sold many of my clothes for bread…. I want many of the common necessaries of life; I am almost always sick…..My health is not only decayed but destroyed… You married me to this man, and as soon as sorrow took hold of me you left me to it. Had you had the same, nay a quarter of the love to me that I have for you, long since you would have been with me; it was in your power – you, who could go to Germany, could you not reach Gainsborough?'

She said if she had committed suicide then her murder would have justly been laid at his door. Only assistance from her other brothers, Samuel and Charles, had saved her from total destruction. And she expressed her hope that John would 'forsake her not in the day of her distress' so she could 'live to see happier days'.

A letter dated 4 August 1740 shows Emily was still alone and dependent on others telling her about John's evangelical activities. Much of what was being said was hostile and so she urged him to explain to her what he and Charles were doing:

'Why do you leave our churches to preach in fields and markets? And what is become of our excellent liturgy, which cannot be used in such places? Then why do you condemn all means of grace except those used by yourselves?'

However, that she was keen to still think well of John is evident. She describes herself as his 'most affectionate sister' and says:

'Our clergy, generally speaking, are unworthy of the sacred office they hold, and if God has raised you up to reform the nation, I heartily wish you prosperity. I believe all the Methodists to be good Christians, though not infallible. May the spirit of truth.... guide us into the truth.'

The letter also shows Emily was still desperate to find somewhere to live. It is probable that by this stage Harpur had deserted her. Her mother was suggesting she might be housed in the school that John was creating in Kingswood. Instead John offered her food and lodging (alongside their mother) in the Foundery, which was the new base he was creating for his work in London. To her dismay what he failed to provide her with when she moved there was much personal attention. His evangelical work always took priority. Emily found this very difficult and accused him of a lack of kindness in scarcely ever speaking to her. She said it was obvious he looked on showing any family affection as a sin and told him: 'Your zeal for God's glory ought not to eat up natural affection'. She also was critical of the fact he belittled her faith simply because she would not immediately sign up to be a Methodist:

'If I be not perfect as the Methodists I am a firm member of the Church of England, and endeavour to practice my known duty.... You ought not to judge me for not holding all you believe.'

Some historians have presented Emily as a demanding and embittered woman but, in fairness to her, she was only saying what other members of the family also said at various times – that John gave his family little of his time. For example, Charles Wesley complained in July 1740 that their mother might as well be dead for any notice John was taking of her.

After their mother's death, John became increasingly angry at what he saw as Emily's ingratitude and her readiness to question some of what he and Charles were doing. She still had issues about their promotion of salvation by faith and she particularly voiced her opposition to John's ideas on Christian perfection. In June 1743 John wrote her a most stinging rebuke. He reminded her that he was housing and feeding her from his limited resources and went on to say:

'You are of all creatures the most unthankful to God and man. I stand amazed at you. How little you have profited under such means of improvement! Surely, whenever your eyes are opened, whenever you see your own tempers, with the advantages you have enjoyed, you will make no scruple to pronounce yourself (whores and murderers not excepted) the very chief of sinners.'

These were harsh words to a woman who only the year before had helped nurse his mother through her final illness.

Emily eventually agreed to become a Methodist and she performed the work of a deaconess, taking up rooms in a house at the side of the Methodist Chapel created in West Street, London. She devoted herself to helping the sick and needy and for a time she also looked after her sister Patty. By 1751 John was obviously on better terms again with her and she welcomed that:

'Is your heart inclined to an union; mine is more so. I embrace your friendship most cordially. Let no cloud henceforth come between us, but may our ancient love revive.'

However, she remained sorrowful that she saw so little of John: 'I want most sadly to see you and…. and enjoy the very great blessing of some hours' converse.' Interestingly she attributed his failure to come to her home as partly a product of his embarrassment at having to introduce his wife to her: 'Alas I am too weak, too low in the world for to bring a new wife to see.'

Emily pined for the days when as a young person she had enjoyed the company of her brothers and sisters, a time when her flesh and blood had shown 'the greatest love and tenderness to each other of any family in Lincolnshire'. She looked forward to death as a time when she might finally come to understand why her subsequent life had been so filled with afflictions. She lived another twenty years, dying at the age of eighty, but her love for John was always greater than his for her. In a letter in 1761 he dismissively referred to her as someone who 'never heartily joined in the work' and he made no reference at all in his journal to her death in 1771.

❑ ❑ ❑ ❑ ❑

2. A WIFE ABUSED

The sad story of Sukey Wesley

Susanna (or Sukey as she was usually called) was the second surviving daughter of the Wesleys. Born in 1695 she developed into a vivacious, pretty, and good-natured girl with a romantic nature and a lively sense of fun. After the 1709 fire destroyed the family home she was temporarily sent away to stay first in Gainsborough and then in the home of her uncle, Matthew Wesley, in London. It is difficult to assess the level of her intelligence from the few letters that have survived, but the fact her mother taught her alongside the highly intelligent Emily may point to her being gifted. So too does the fact that, while she was away, her mother sent her a complicated treatise on the Apostle's Creed, saying:

"Susanna Wesley"

'You know how very well I love you… which regard I cannot better express than by endeavouring to instill into your mind those principles of knowledge and virtue that are absolutely necessary in order to your leading a good life…. I shall earnestly beseech Almighty God to enlighten your mind, to renew and sanctify you by His Holy Spirit'.

This was followed by the commencement of a second composition (this time on the ten commandments) in 1711. She told Sukey that it was no good just learning her creed and catechism by heart or saying a few prayers morning and night: 'You must understand what you say, and you must practise what you know'.

In 1712 Susanna Wesley bemoaned the fact that all her children had learnt bad habits whilst away from her watchful eye:

'In those [homes] they were left at full liberty to converse with servants…. and to run abroad to play with any children, good or bad. They soon learned to neglect a strict observance of the Sabbath; and got knowledge of several songs and bad things…. [Their] civil behavior ….was in a great measure lost and a clownish accent and many rude ways were learnt'.

Sukey would have been no exception, not least because she went to London with her younger sister, Hetty, the most rebellious and outspoken of Susanna's daughters. Returning to Epworth after the delights of London must have been very difficult.

Their father Samuel was clearly concerned at the way his attractive daughters were attracting the attentions of young men. Indeed when the Rectory appeared to be suffering from strange noises in December 1716 he at first attributed this to unwelcome suitors coming to the house at night for clandestine meetings. Only reluctantly did he and his wife eventually conclude the house was genuinely haunted. Sukey wrote to her brother Samuel about what was happening and obviously found it very amusing. Here, for example, is her account of the poltergeist making a plate move:

'Last Sunday, to my father's no small amazement, his trencher danced upon the table a pretty while, without anybody's stirring the table. When lo! An adventurous wretch took it up and spoiled the sport, for it remained still ever after.'

Shortly afterwards Sukey returned to London, this time to stay with her wealthy if rather eccentric uncle, Samuel Annesley. He was very taken with his lively niece and Sukey understandably lived in the hope that he might provide her with a dowry to attract an appropriate husband. In the event he went off to pursue his commercial interests in India without doing anything for her and so Sukey was faced with the prospect of returning home to the poverty of Epworth. To avoid this fate she married without her parents' consent a wealthy farmer called Richard Ellison in 1719. It proved a tragic mistake. Though he had money he was not a gentleman but coarse and rather brutal. In January 1722 Susanna complained to her brother that his unkind treatment had led Sukey to 'rashly throw herself away upon a man that is little inferior to the apostate angels in wickedness'. She described Ellison as Sukey's 'plague' and as 'a constant affliction to the family', and said the grief she had faced in losing ten of her children was nothing compared to what she felt over Sukey's ill-treatment.

Sukey was not one to particularly confide her feelings to her brothers or sisters and she did not therefore, as far as we know, write about her marital problems. However, the few comments that have survived from other members of the family all depict 'Dick' Ellison in a bad light. Both her brother Samuel and her sister Martha claimed Ellison had nothing to commend him but his money because he possessed 'neither religion, birth… nor good nature'. Her father wrote about how he would rather take horrible medicine than spend time in his company. Her sister Kezzy described how troubled she was by the constant quarrelling between Sukey and her husband. And the full extent of their marital disharmony is revealed in a letter written in 1730 by Patty Wesley:

'Dick is (if possible) tenfold more the child of Hell than he used to be. He took it into his head the other night almost to beat out his wife's brains.'

Richard Ellison almost certainly was a man who became violent when drunk. On this occasion a servant had rebelled and hit back. When Sukey tried to intervene she was brutally beaten. Not surprisingly, whenever Sukey and her husband visited Epworth the rest of the family experienced, in the words of Kezzy, 'a constant uneasiness'.

Sukey did not feel she could leave her husband because they had four children in fairly rapid succession: John, Ann, Deborah, and Richard. The Wesleys did what little they could to support them. Indeed Susanna was almost killed when she insisted on travelling through a snowstorm to assist Sukey recover from a particularly difficult childbirth. Similarly, Emily showed her love by leaving her employment in Lincoln to nurse her during a life-threatening illness. In 1735 John Wesley contemplated whether he should take Sukey and possibly her children with him to America. His brother Samuel Wesley said he did not blame him for thinking of taking such action because with such a father 'her children…in all probability in a few years may want conversion as much as those poor people you are going among'.

The wealth that had originally attracted Sukey did not last because Ellison made a number of business mistakes. When a fire entirely destroyed their home, Sukey left him and sought refuge for herself and her children in London. It has been surmised that her departure may have arisen because he started the fire whilst drunk, but equally it may simply have been that she could no longer take his violence. Sukey was fortunate in that John and Charles Wesley were able to offer her help with accommodation. Richard Ellison was determined he would get her back. To that end he advertised his own death, knowing Sukey would return to attend his funeral. One can only imagine her shock at finding him waiting for her! She escaped again and this time went into hiding so he could not find her.

Matters went from bad to worse for Ellison. He was financially ruined when faulty drains led to all his land being flooded for two years. This destroyed all his cows and all his horses bar one. John Wesley had to resort to using the services of his banking friend, Ebeneezer Blackwell, in order to obtain money for Ellison from a fund created by a Mr Butterfield. Ellison appears to have been so moved by this kind act that he began to reform, attending services at the Foundery and eventually becoming a Methodist. However, Sukey never returned to him. Nevertheless, Charles Wesley arranged for Ellison's burial when he died in April 1760:

'He told me he was not afraid to die, and believed God, for Christ's sake, had forgive him. I felt a most solemn awe while I committed his body to the earth'.

Sukey's elder son, John, became a Customs and Excise officer in Bristol whilst the younger, Richard, died in his twenties. Her daughters both married French Protestant refugees. The elder, Ann, married Pierre le Lièvre who was educated at the school in Kingswood created by John Wesley. He was ordained and became a vicar in Lutterworth in Leicestershire. The younger daughter Deborah married Pierre Collet, a silkweaver in London. Sukey appears to have spent most of her later life with Ann, who, after becoming a widow, married a man called Gaunt. Sukey died in Ann's home in 1764 and her brother John wrote of this to Charles:

'Sister Sukey was in huge agonies for five days, and then died in full assurance of faith. Some of her last words (after she had been speechless for some time) were, 'Jesus is come! Heaven is here!'

Hogarth portrays the evils of drink in 'Beer Street'

3. A FAMILY SCANDAL

The heart-breaking story of Hetty Wesley

Mehetabel (known as Hetty) was born in 1697 or 1698 and she was the first daughter to actually be born at Epworth. She was the most beautiful and witty and fun-loving of the sisters, but also the most headstrong. Her later memories of her early childhood were of happily enjoying her mother's lessons and her sisters' company:

> 'Learning here placed her richer stores in view,
> Or, winged with love, the minutes gaily flew….
> We wandered innocent through sylvan scenes,
> Or tripped like fairies o'er the level greens….
> Youth, wit, good nature, candour, sense, combined
> To serve, delight, and civilise mankind'.

It was Hetty who was the first to awake during the famous Epworth fire in 1709 and who roused the rest of the family, so ensuring their escape. Afterwards she and her elder sister Sukey were sent to temporarily stay in London with their uncle, Matthew Wesley. The experience made a return to isolated and backward Epworth hateful. She described it in verse as a place 'debarred of wisdom, wit, and grace' and its inhabitants as 'asses dull, on dunghills born… a sordid race.' It may well have been Hetty who in a moment of frustrated boredom invented the ghost that so disturbed her parents and her other sisters in the winter of 1716, though this cannot be proved.

Because she was highly intelligent, she was possibly educated to a higher level than that of the other sisters, being proficient in Latin and Greek by the age of nine. This made her useful to her father because she could help him in his writings. It has even been suggested that one of his best verses (a poem called 'Eupolis' Hymn to the Creator') was based on lines first produced by her. Her usefulness may have been a factor in why he was particularly reluctant to see her married or he may simply have viewed her as being too willful to make a sensible choice of husband. She feared she might end up as a spinster given her isolated existence and what she called her father's 'sour-faced' attitude towards any potential suitor, and she tried to persuade her mother to intervene to help her 'distressed daughter'.

In 1724 Samuel and Susanna moved into the inferior parsonage of Wroot and rented out the Epworth rectory to their daughter Sukey and her husband. Hetty was packed off to serve as a lady companion and governess to a family called the Granthams in the town of Kelstern, which was about thirty miles from

Epworth. A factor in this decision may have been that Samuel judged Hetty was showing too much interest in John Romley, the handsome son of the local schoolmaster in Wroot and Samuel's designated curate.

In Kelstern Hetty was courted by a local lawyer called Will Atkins, who appeared to her to be both clever and respectable. However, her father hated lawyers and told her Atkins was inappropriate because he was 'unprincipled'. It came hard to the twenty-seven year old Hetty to be denied what she saw as a desirable marriage. In desperation she agreed in July to elope with Atkins and the two of them subsequently travelled to London. Unfortunately, once Atkins had had sex with her, he refused to marry her. Heart-broken, Hetty returned home rather than live in sin. Inevitably she faced the wrath of her parents, especially Samuel. On 2 August he wrote to John of the terrible shock suffered by Susanna when she heard what had happened and said that, as far as he was concerned, 'this day [I have] lost [Hetty] though she's not so well as dead'. The outraged Samuel felt he could never forgive his daughter for what she had done and, in another letter to John, again commented 'she is lost to me'. In his anger he claimed her behaviour had always been suspect: 'I've had little hopes of her.... since she has been half a year old'. In the words of the historian Frederick Maser, Hetty's 'open immorality was a stench to his soul'.

One early researcher into Hetty's life asserted that Atkins might have married Hetty when he discovered she was pregnant, but her father 'interfered to prevent their marriage'. Whilst she vowed that he alone would remain the man of her choice, she was force to accept that she would have to marry someone who had her parents' approval. Samuel looked to find her a husband so he could avoid the scandal of his daughter becoming an unmarried mother. It may have been his daughter Nancy's future husband, John Lambert, who suggested a glazier and plumber called William Wright, who was then resident in Lincoln but whose parents lived in the nearby town of Louth. He and Wright were drinking companions.

William Wright was a decent man but he was not well-educated and intellectually he was far Hetty's inferior. It is said only her crippled sister Molly had the courage to try to prevent such an unequal match, telling her father:

'You are seldom kind and rarely just... You are a tyrant to those you love; and now in your tyranny you are going to do... a downright wickedness'.

Hetty did as her father demanded and married William on 13 October 1725 in the nearby town of Haxey. There is no record whether any of her family attended. Only Molly seems to have spent time with her, helping her to come to terms with what had happened. Hetty felt it was a sin to have made vows to a man she did not love. What made the situation worse was that it soon became clear that her new husband had a tendency towards heavy drinking. Though he was a decent man when sober, he was violent when drunk. Hetty was years later to voice her thoughts on marriage in a bitter poem:

> 'That wretch, if such a wretch there be,
> Who hopes for happiness from thee,
> May search successfully as well
> For truth in whores and ease in hell.'

Neither of her parents came to see her and eventually it was a heavily pregnant Hetty who made the effort to try and effect a reconciliation. Her father refused to see her and he persuaded her mother and some of her sisters to believe that any repentance she might be showing was undoubtedly just feigned. In the circumstances it is not surprising that Hetty's baby daughter, who was baptized on 18 February 1726, proved frail and died long before the year was out. When Wright's business affairs took a downturn that summer, it was only the kindness of her sister Nancy that prevented Hetty becoming homeless. She and Wright were invited to stay with them.

The summer of 1726 saw the family taking sides over what had happened. Emily, whose own love life had been wrecked, was not sympathetic towards her erring sister's position, but John Wesley took up Hetty's cause when he returned home from Oxford. That may have been easier for him because he was already in dispute with his father over another issue. Although he was ordained, John was refusing to abandon his career in Oxford in order to become Samuel's curate. On 28 August 1726 John invited all the family to hear

A romantic image of elopement

Samuel Wesley

him preach at Wroot and he spoke on 'charity due to wicked persons'. The motive was not lost on his mother, who told him: 'You wrote this sermon for Hetty'. Samuel Wesley was not amused, not least because he feared John was too lax in his own sexual behaviour. John had recently become a fellow of Lincoln College and it was a condition of that fellowship that he should not marry, but John's looks and character made him attractive to women and he loved flirting with them. This did not go unnoticed by Samuel.

Samuel encouraged both of his other sons to remonstrate with John for defending immorality. He told Charles, who had accompanied John back to Epworth: 'Every day you see how he contradicts me and take's your sister's part before my face'. Charles was in a difficult position. He liked Hetty but he dared not risk his father's displeasure. Though he had just come top in his final exams and won a King's scholarship to Christ Church College, Oxford, he had yet to obtain his father's commitment to fund him at university. He therefore encouraged John to let the matter drop. Samuel was delighted and it may have been no coincidence that he then decided to pay for Charles to go to Oxford, even though the family finances could not afford it.

Samuel also wrote to his eldest son, Samuel, and asked him to add his weight in making John abandon Hetty's defense. His son wisely sought to find out the full facts first and John wrote to him:

'My sister Hetty's behaviour has...been innocent enough since her marriage...[but our father is] inconceivably exasperated against her... and never spoke of her in my hearing but with the utmost detestation...[My] sermon was to endeavour...to convince them... some tenderness was due to her still.'

In fact John's sermon did have one positive outcome. It made Susanna decide to visit her erring daughter, though it was not until October that she finally received Samuel's reluctant permission to do this. She wrongly took this to mean he was 'as well disposed to be reconciled to her as man can be'. Unfortunately, she found Hetty emotionally drained in the aftermath of having lost her infant child, and therefore Hetty greeted her arrival 'without the least emotion of joy or grief' and listened to her 'with great indifference...

[seeming] not pleased that I supposed she stood in need of my pardon'. Susanna later confided:

'I then proposed a reconciliation between her and Mr. Wesley and...she told me she had no desire to see him, because she knew he would reproach her with what was past, and that she could not bear ... I returned home strangely mortified, neither pleased with her nor myself.'

Sadly she concluded the time was not right to try and persuade her husband to forgive Hetty:

'I verily believe that I could by a few words speaking reconcile him to her, but God forbid those few words should be spoken by me till she is better disposed. What her inward frame of mind is, is best known to the searcher of hearts, to whose mercy I leave her, beseeching him to give her true repentance, without which I desire to see her face no more'.

A golden opportunity was thus lost. However, despite this unhappy meeting, measures were set in place by other family members to give Hetty assistance. Her brother Samuel offered her what limited financial support he could, confiding in John that he wished his mother and sister Emily were heartily reconciled to Hetty and that he was resolved to change the attitude of their father. Her uncle Matthew Wesley was similarly sympathetic to her situation and he paid to set up her husband in his own business in Frith Street in the Soho area of London so he could see more of her and she would not be dependant on Nancy's charity. Once she was in London, Charles showed his support by visiting her 'almost continuously' for a week. He never told his father about this, confiding his visits only to his brother John:

'Poor sister Hetty!... In a little neat room she had hired did the good-natured, ingenuous, contented creature watch, and I talk, over a few short days which we both wished had been longer. As yet she lives pretty well...though I fancy there is another [child] coming. Brother Sam and sister are very kind to her, and I hope will continue so... She begs you write to her.'

Hetty was indeed pregnant again and she returned to Louth so she could have her baby in the home of Wright's parents. On this occasion her father did go to see her but it was not a happy meeting. The only comment we have about what happened is by Patty Wesley in a letter dated 7 February 1727. She wrote it was fortunate Hetty was 'brought to bed' because it stopped Samuel saying 'what he otherwise might have said to her'. Her father's implacable refusal to forgive her weighed heavily with Hetty, not least because he expressed no sorrow when her second child only survived a few days. Her despair was deepened further by the death of a third child, three days after its birth, on 28 September 1728. She dictated to Wright a poem about her feelings and he sent a copy to her brother John, who corrected Wright's misspellings and had it published. Its opening lines were:

> 'Tender softness! Infant mild!
> Perfect, purest, brightest child!
> Transient lustre! Beauteous clay!
> Smiling wonder of a day!
> Ere the last convulsive start
> Rend thy unresisting heart…
> Ah, regard a mother's moan,
> Anguish deeper than thy own!'

Hetty partially attributed the death of her third child to the noxious fumes emanating from the white lead used in her husband's business but she also feared it might be a product of living under her father's curse. She urged him to forgive her saying that her brothers would all 'report to you what they have seen of my way of life and my daily struggle to redeem the past'. She also reminded him of his own role in marrying her to Wright: 'As you planted my matrimonial bliss, so you cannot run away from my prayer when I beseech you to water it with a little kindness.' It was to no avail. Samuel had not entirely thrown off his strict Puritanical upbringing and Christian duty ranked higher in his thinking than Christian forgiveness.

By this stage three dead children were not Hetty's only source of grief. John Lambert had also set himself up in business in London. At one level this had been welcomed because it enabled her to see Nancy regularly, but unfortunately the friendship between the sisters' respective husbands had ill consequences. Both men encouraged each other to drink too much and, in Wright's case, he began to neglect his business and to regularly physically abuse Hetty. Outwardly, of course, William was still a respectable man of business and in a letter to her father in July 1729 Hetty felt she could only hint at what was happening in her marriage, not least because Samuel viewed Wright with immense favour for having married her while she was bearing an illegitimate child. She informed him that she could not help feeling that it had been a sin to marry a man with whom she had nothing in common and for whom she had had no affection. Craving her father's forgiveness, she added she would try to bear her fate with fortitude:

'I could say much more, but would rather eternally stifle my sentiments than have the torment of thinking they agree not with yours…. Since upon some accounts I am happier than I deserve, it is best to say little of things quite past remedy, and endeavour, as I really do, to make myself more and more contented…. I am not more than human…. [but] I sincerely promise never more to offend you by saying too much'.

The woman who had once taken pride in her wit, also vowed to please her father by promising to be 'as little witty as possible' – a task made easy by her current lifestyle.

Susanna Wesley still felt constrained by her husband's attitude and she did not feel able to comfort Hetty. In 1731 she confided to John: 'I hope better of her than some others do'. It was the nearest she came to saying her husband was wrong. Denied parental support, Hetty found some release in confiding her real 'deep anguish of spirit' to God:

>'Oppressed with utmost weight of woe,
>Debarred of freedom, health and rest;
>What human eloquence can show
>The inward anguish of my breast!...
>Enable me to bear my lot,
>O thou who only can redress:
>Eternal God! Forsake me not
>In this extreme of my distress.'

As far as Hetty was concerned, her wedding vow made it essential to view Wright as her God-given master. He was the person 'on whom my earthly bliss depends'. Aware that he could be remorseful after he had struck her, she confided her sorrow in a long poem intended only for his eyes. In it she voiced her impatience at the way she was being treated and yet her desire to make him 'throw his cold neglect aside' only by using 'saddest, softest strains':

>'If e'er thou didst in Hetty see
>Aught fair, or good, or dear to thee,
>If gentle speech can ever move
>The cold remains of former love,
>Turn thee at last – my bosom ease,
>Or tell me why I cease to please'.

She felt his ill-treatment could not arise from her having lost her beauty because she still retained that:

>'Is it because revolving tears,
>Heart-breaking sighs, and fruitless tears,
>Have quite deprived this form of mine
>Of all that once thou fancied fine?
>Ah no! what once allured thy sight
>Is still in its meridian height.
>These eyes their usual lustre show
>When uneclipsed by flowing woe.
>Old age and wrinkles in this face
>As yet could never find a place....
>Nor does this slighted bosom show
>The thousand hours it spends in woe'.

Nor could his brutality arise from her manner to him:

> Or is it that, oppressed with care,
> I stun with loud complaints thine ear;
> And make thy home for quiet meant
> The seat of noise and discontent?
> Ah no! those ears were ever free
> From matrimonial melody:
> For though thine absence I lament
> When half the lonely night is spent,
> Yet when the watch or early morn
> Has brought me hopes of thy return,
> I oft have wiped these watchful eyes,
> Concealed my cares, and curbed my sighs,
> In spite of grief, to let thee see
> I wore an endless smile for thee'.

It was therefore his pleasure in drinking that was the root cause of their domestic unhappiness:

> 'To some obscure, unclean retreat,
> With fiends incarnate glad to meet,
> The vile companions of thy mirth,
> The scum and refuse of the earth;
> Who, when inspired by beer, can grin
> At witless oaths and jests obscene...
> While thou, in raptures, with stretched jaws
> Crownest each joke with loud applause'.

The poem ends with challenging Wright to let her know whether there was any point in trying to stay together:

> 'Unkind, ungrateful as thou art,
> Say, must I ne'er regain thy heart?
> Must all attempts to please thee prove
> Unable to regain thy love?'

If that was the case, it were better she were dead because she could not bear his contempt:

> 'To thee thy liberty restore
> To laugh when Hetty is no more'.

As far as we know, Hetty had at least two more children who did not survive infancy. She grew much closer to her uncle Matthew, who enjoyed her company. He, unlike her father, was totally prepared to forgive her mistake in eloping with Atkins. She sometimes visited Matthew in his home and on one occasion she even had her husband's permission to accompany her uncle on a trip to the spa towns of Bath and Tunbridge. It was probably through Matthew's contacts that Hetty's skill as a poet was recognized and some of her verse eventually appeared in 'The Gentleman's Magazine' (and, years later, in various other magazines, including, 'The Poetical Register', 'The Christian Magazine", and 'The Arminian Magazine'). William Wright appears to have shown little interest in her visits to her uncle and he was probably unaware when, in 1736, one of her admirers wrote about the beauty of both her form and mind in 'The Gentleman's Magazine':

> "Twere difficult with portrait just to trace
> The blooming beauties of her lovely face;
> The roseate bloom that blushes on her chek;
> Her eyes, whence rays of pointed lightning break;
> Each brow the bow of Cupid, whence her darts
> With certain archery strike unguarded hearts;
> Her lips, that with a rubied tincture glow,
> Soft as the soothing sounds which from them flow.
> But Oh! What words, what numbers shall I find
> T'express the boundless treasures of her mind,
> Where wit and judgement spread their copious mines,
> And every grace and every virtue shines!'

In 1737 Hetty personally nursed her uncle Matthew through what proved his final illness and he died in her arms. He left her £200 in his will and a further £100 for her child Amelia (who did not survive infancy).

By then two other significant family deaths had occurred. One was the death of her sister Molly in 1734. As she had been the only family member to oppose her marriage to Wright, Hetty felt her loss deeply and wrote a poem in her honour. The other death was that of her father Samuel in 1735, still unreconciled with her. To the end he doubted the sincerity of her repentance. Happily his departure freed Susanna Wesley to be more supportive to Hetty, especially when she came to live in London and took up residence at the Foundery in London. After ten years Hetty finally experienced a full reconciliation with her mother. Her sister Emily also appears to have become much friendlier towards her after their father's death. This new family support compensated for the loss of not only her uncle but also of her eldest brother Samuel in 1738.

Susanna's last years were happy ones because the divisions within the family were over. The whole family was united in grief when Susanna died in the summer of 1742. By this time Hetty had clearly become a supporter of the evangelistic work of her brothers John and Charles. However, in a letter to John written in 1743 Hetty clearly felt wary of publicly owning herself to be a Methodist because of Wright's hostility towards what her brothers were doing:

'I never confessed so powerfully as I ought how entirely I was of your mind, because I was taxed with insincerity and hypocrisy whenever I opened my mouth in favour of religion, or owned how great things God had done for me.... Though I am cut off from all human help or ministry....[I am] satisfied with nothing else than God.... I dare not desire health, only patience, resignation, and the spirit of an healthful mind'.

Wright had always been socially and intellectually out of his depth with the Wesleys and for a time he appears to have banned Hetty from attending any Methodist meetings. However, he appears to have eventually relented and permitted this. He even gave Hetty hope that he might begin seeking his own salvation.

By this stage she had lost her looks and was in very poor health, partly because of the impact of constantly living alongside her husband's lead works and partly because of her sad life:

> 'Grief has my blood and spirits drunk,
> My tears do like the night-dew fall;
> My cheeks are faded, eyes are sunk,
> And all my draughts are dash'd with gall'.

John and Charles arranged for her to go to Bristol where she could receive medical treatment at its spa. She lodged with a Mrs. Vigour, a member of the society based at the New Room, and was treated by her and others with great kindness, showering on her 'all manner of courtesy'. It is clear that she looked to Charles with immense gratitude for his care of her. He was quite keen for her to take on a role among the women within the society, but Hetty felt this was inappropriate, possibly because she still felt scarred by the scandal of her earlier life. She told John that, though she wished she could be better employed, she feared she might bring 'still more disgrace' upon them.

Though she returned to London in the autumn of 1745, her health was still very frail. In a letter to Charles she refers to herself as having to keep to her bed because she was suffering from 'a violent cough' and how she had become a living skeleton with 'my bones.... ready to come through my skin'. On her spiritual condition she wrote:

'I have no sense of God's presence, ever since I took my bed..... [but] I enjoy so great a measure of quietness and thankfulness as is really above nature. Hallelujah!.... I am perfectly easy and resigned... [to my death because I have given up my life] with dear Will's spiritual welfare and all other things to the sovereign Physician of souls and bodies.... I cannot say I desire life a minute longer.... Pray join in prayer with me that... [my husband] may persevere'.

The Hotwells in Bristol, where Hetty recuperated

Her gratitude that her suffering was nearing its end was voiced in verse:

> 'While sickness rends the tenement of clay,
> the approaching change with pleasure I survey....
> No longer shall I bear, my friends to please,
> The hard constraint of seeming much at ease;
> Wearing an outward smile, a look serene,
> While piercing racks and tortures work within.
> Yet let me not, ungrateful to my God,
> Record the evil, and forget the good'.

Surprisingly the bed-bound Hetty survived five more years. One of the early Methodists described her as being obviously 'a broken-hearted woman' but one who was still elegant and refined in manner and who still bore the traces of having once been beautiful. She had hoped to meet death with joy but in the event the extent of her pain and her physical debilitation prevented this. Charles referred to her as 'a gracious, tender, trembling soul; a bruised reed which the Lord will not break'. He visited her three times in March 1750, the last being on the 21st. He comforted her as she lay dying with the words:

'Thy sun shall no more go down, neither shall thy moon withdraw itself; for the Lord shall be thine everlasting light, and the days of thy mourning shall be ended'.

He openly wept as he attended her funeral a week later. He also recorded that her husband was 'inconsolable'. This may explain why Hetty's sister Martha for a time went to stay with him and acted as his housekeeper. However, this did not prevent Wright subsequently remarrying.

Charles was not to see Wright again until Wright asked him to attend his deathbed in 1755. He wrote:

'His stubborn heart was much softened by the approach of death. Now he is a poor sinner indeed, full of horror and condemnation, yet not without hope of mercy. I prayed again with my poor penitent.... [He] expressed a hope and an earnest desire for one, only one thing – for the voice of a trumpet to warn all mankind not to walk in the paths wherein he had walked.... I prayed with confidence for a Christless, dying sinner'.

It is not clear when Wright actually died but it was sometime between then and 1759. The story of his ill-fated marriage became the basis of the novel 'Hetty Wesley' written by Arthur Quiller-Couch in 1904.

The final word is best left to Hetty who, before she died, wrote her own epitaph:

> 'Destined while living to sustain
> An equal share of grief and pain....
> Without complaint she learned to bear
> A living death, a long despair...
> The painful mortal combat's o'er;
> A broken heart can bleed no more!'

4. A CRIPPLE IN SEARCH OF LOVE

The unhappy story of Molly Wesley

Mary (or Molly as she was called) Wesley was born at South Ormesby in 1696. Although she had a very pretty face with a beautiful white complexion, she lacked the figure to match it. Not long after her birth she was seriously injured, possibly as a result of the careless behaviour of a servant, and so she grew up seriously deformed and stunted in her growth. Despite her physical disabilities, she was still expected to contribute to the running of the household but she was unable to participate in any of the lighter fun moments enjoyed by her brothers and sisters. She felt they did not love her and developed a strong inferiority complex. The extent of her unhappiness is revealed in a letter to John Wesley in January 1726 in which she told him she fully understood why he did not bother writing to her:

'I have not the good hap to be one of your favourite sisters... [and] I am sensible nothing I can say will add either to your pleasure or profit....Why should I wonder at any indifference shown to such a despicable person as myself, seeing I am conscious there is nothing in my composition that merits esteem?.... God has cut me off from the pleasurable parts of life, and rendered me incapable of attracting the love of my relations.... I have always been the jest of the family'.

She similarly wrote to her brother Charles, who viewed her as 'a patient grizzle' (i.e. grumbler):

'I think I may say I have lived in a state of affliction ever since I was born, being the ridicule of mankind and the reproach of my family'.

Remarkably Molly was not embittered by her experience because she also told him that, although she found it difficult 'to be serviceable to my friends, and particularly to my relatives' this did not stop her wishing she could help people: 'I should be glad if I could... to spend my whole life in doing good to my fellow-creatures'.

In 1727 the family's financial position was so dire that it was decided to put Molly 'to trade' despite her infirmity. The following year her father wrote to John Wesley how Molly had 'miraculously' gained employment to help the family finances and 'given the first fruits of her earnings to her mother....[while also] presenting her with a new cloak of her own buying and making'.

Molly's experience of feeling isolated and rejected may explain why she was the first to speak out courageously against her father's ill treatment of her sister Hetty. In 1727 her willingness to defend the under-dog also led her to befriend a young impoverished lad called John Whitelamb. He had been brought to live with the family because her father had recognized that he had the intelligence and natural skill to act both as a copyist and as an engraver of illustrations for a book Samuel was writing on Job. Whitelamb came from a very poor family but had shown his potential at the charity school that existed in Wroot. Initially Whitelamb was very glad to live with 'so pious a family', but he soon realized he was being used. Samuel gave him no money for the work he was doing and made little attempt to further educate him (other than the basic Greek and Latin that he required to undertake his duties). Tall and gangly and dressed in rags, 'poor starveling Johnny' (as Susanna called him) was often the butt of Samuel's humour and this led him to be also 'deprecated and reviled by every common servant'. Only Molly was truly kind to him and increasingly she helped him with the work he was undertaking for her father.

In 1728 Whitelamb saved Samuel from a possible drowning when he was involved in a serious ferry accident. Initially this brought little improvement to his treatment. In 1730, for example, he complained to Susanna about his 'poor and wretched condition' and that he could have learnt more in one month than he had in three years 'if I'd had books'. He said he was tired of being subjected to Samuel's 'satirical wit' and saw little chance of being properly paid or receiving any 'future advantage'. However, Whitelamb's action in saving Samuel may partially explain why the family belatedly decided it would help pay for Whitelamb to undertake a degree at Lincoln College, Oxford, where John Wesley was a tutor. Whitelamb agreed he would attempt to live off just three pence a day and John Wesley and his brother Samuel agreed to fund some clothes for him.

There is no doubt that Whitelamb worked very hard to justify the opportunity he had been unexpectedly given. In 1731 John Wesley wrote:

'He reads one English, one Latin, and one Greek book alternately.... If he goes on as he has begun, I dare take upon me to say that by the time he has been here four or five years, there will not be such a one of his standing in Lincoln College, perhaps not in the University of Oxford'.

Self-advancement was not the only motivation behind his efforts. Whitelamb wanted to prove he was worthy of marrying Molly, who had so supported and befriended him. The fact she was fourteen years older than him and crippled was immaterial as far as he was concerned. While at Epworth in the summer of 1733 he asked her to marry him and she agreed. Lacking as yet parental assent this was what was termed a pre-engagement. It was probably no coincidence that Whitelamb took the decision to become a member of the Oxford Methodists on his return to the university – the step was bound to win him greater favour with Molly's family.

However, Molly was not the only woman in Whitelamb's life. In September a fellow student called William Smith informed John Wesley that his protégé was having an affair with a woman called 'Miss Betty'. John investigated and learned 'all' before confronting Whitelamb. Almost certainly he pointed out to him that his behaviour was not only incompatible with his supposed love for Molly but also with his expressed wish to be ordained. It may not have been coincidence that in a sermon he was writing at this time John wrote: 'Many loves may consist in the same heart… but two ultimate loves are as flat a contradiction as two first or two lasts'. We do not know what explanation Whitelamb gave John but many years later he told Charles Wesley it had been an indiscretion caused by 'a heat of youthful blood and want of experience in the world'.

John determined he must inform Molly and travelled to Epworth. There he first confided what he knew to his sister Kezzy and she confirmed that Molly had to be told. It has been suggested that Kezzy wanted to stop her sister marrying Whitelamb because she fancied him herself, but there is absolutely no evidence to support such a surmise. She was justly shocked by Whitelamb's betrayal of her sister. Kezzy told Molly and Molly then told her mother. Susanna was horrified by such 'a notorious violation of his promises' and subsequently reprimanded John for not telling her immediately about 'the looseness' of Whitelamb's principles and his 'disreputable practices'.

Epworth Church

While John Wesley was away from Oxford, Whitelamb was ordained as a deacon. When John returned, he and Charles had further discussions with their potential brother-in-law on 8 October. Whitelamb must have won them over because they let him return to Epworth as their father's curate. However, he still had to face Susanna's wrath. She was not amused when 'he was not much moved' by her intervention. She told him if he did not write and end all relationship with 'his new doxy' then she 'would immediately send Molly away, where he should never see her more'. It was only Molly's obvious determination to marry that made her mother accept the wedding should proceed. Though she described the marriage as being 'full sore against my will', she did not tell her husband what had happened. In that way she enabled Molly to have the man she wanted.

In ignorance Samuel Wesley happily married the couple on 21 December 1733. Afterwards Susanna wrote to her son John:

'[I] only laboured what I could to dissuade Molly from it. But the flesh and the evil were too hard for me. I could not prevail. Yet with God nothing is impossible, and though this unequal marriage has to me a terrible aspect, 'tis possible for God to bring good out of this great evil... She thinks she can reform what is amiss in him. I think myself he grows more serious and regular.'

Kezzy did not share her optimism. She was sure her sister had thrown herself away on an immoral man who had 'very little sense of religion according to our notions'. She informed John that Whitelamb was not at all contrite about his affair in Oxford and had actually boasted to her about what had taken place. She criticized her brother for 'the unwise choice you made of a friend' and advised John to make sure that Whitelamb's 'doxy' in Oxford knew about the marriage. She feared otherwise the two might renew their relationship. She expressed her feelings over the wedding in no uncertain terms, saying Whitelamb was no better than Dick Ellison or William Wright:

'Our rejoicing [at a wedding] is always turned into mourning, because we cannot meet with an honest man.... I used all the little rhetoric I was mistress of to dissuade her from marrying, but it was all in vain'.

Not surprisingly Whitelamb came to hate Kezzy and he attempted to blacken her name with one of her potential suitors, Westley Hall, who was also training to become a clergyman.

On 14 January 1734 Samuel Wesley formally requested to the Lord Chancellor that the living at Wroot be transferred from him to Whitelamb, describing him as:

'a valuable person, of uncommon brightness, learning, piety, and indefatiguable industry.... For the truth of his character I will be answerable to God and man'.

It was not a wonderful post because Wroot was a dismal and waterlogged place that was accessible only by boat for part of the year, but Samuel recognized that Molly and her husband were more than content to make it their home. He told the Lord Chancellor: 'They love the place, though I can get nobody else to reside on it'. When Molly became almost immediately pregnant, Kezzy regretted her outspoken opposition to Whitelamb because it made it difficult for her to help her sister. In July she told John:

'Mr. Whitelamb and I grow more indifferent than ever, nor can I think of what way I must take to reconcile us. He will scarce speak if we meet. I would not choose to live as enemies, but if he will, I can't help it.'

In October Molly gave birth to a stillborn child on 28 October after a very difficult labour. The apothecary in attendance was Robert Harper. It was obvious her life was in danger but John Wesley, who was at Epworth at the time, did not visit Molly after the day of her delivery. He seems to have been more concerned to talk to his other sisters about the desirability of celibacy! Not surprisingly he found them 'very cold' towards him. John departed back to Oxford on the morning of 31 October and that afternoon Molly died. When he heard the news John wrote a funeral sermon 'for Molly'. We do not have a copy of this but a long poem written by Hetty has survived. It was written to the memory of her 'tenderest, dearest, fairest friend' and concluded with the following praise for her sister's virtues:

John Wesley preaching on his father's tomb in Epworth in 1742

> 'To soundest prudence (life's unerring guide),
> To love sincere, religion without pride;
> To friendship perfect in a female mind,
> Which I nor hope nor wish on earth to find;
> To mirth (the balm of care) from lightness free,
> Unblemished faith, unwearied industry;
> To every charm and grace combined in you,
> Sister and friend – a long and last adieu.'

If her siblings had not treated her very well in her youth, in hindsight they recognized her qualities and they all now emphasized their sorrow at her loss. Her sisters spoke of her loving, generous and honest nature and her brothers said she had 'a mind and disposition almost angelic'. Hearing all this it is not surprising that the first researcher into the Wesley family erroneously concluded that she must have been 'the favourite and delight of the whole family'.

Whitelamb by all accounts was genuinely devastated at Molly's death. John Wesley suggested he should consider accompanying him abroad on missionary work to take his mind off his grief, but this offer was eventually declined because Whitelamb could not get permission to leave his parish. He remained at Wroot for thirty-five years but all the members of the Wesley family had little or nothing to do with him. It is probable that they never forgave him for his behaviour before the wedding and simply saw him as the cause of Molly's death, though his refusal to accept John's evangelical activities undoubtedly also contributed to his isolation.

When John visited Epworth to preach in 1742, Whitelamb came to hear him but feared to make himself known. Afterwards he wrote to John that, although he could not agree with him on some matters, he could not help still loving him because he had been 'more than a father' to him in Oxford:

'I retain the highest veneration and affection for you... My heart overflows with gratitude; I feel in a higher degree all that tenderness and yearning of bowels with which I am affected towards every branch of Mr Wesley's family.... [Yet] I am quite forgot. None of the family ever honour me with a line.... I have been passionate, fickle, a fool; but I hope I shall never be ungrateful.... Glad I should be that you would make use of me'.

No use was ever made of him. John Wesley clearly dismissed him as a man lacking in sincerity and integrity. Whitelamb never embraced Methodism and, according to Wesley, he was a useless clergyman who lacked a true faith and consequently moved first towards Deism and then towards Catholicism. John's harsh comment on his death was: 'Oh why did he not die forty years ago while he knew in whom he believed'. This judgement is unfair because it is clear that when Whitelamb died in July 1769 he was held in high regard by his parishioners and nearby fellow clergy.

5. HAPPY OR NOT?

The story of Nancy Wesley

Anne (known as Nancy) Wesley was born with a twin brother on 17 May 1701. Seven months later her twin died. We know less about Nancy than any of her sisters. A reference in one of Susanna's letters indicates she thought Nancy and Molly were the least intelligent of her daughters. However, the only clear information we have about Nancy's early life is a description of how she was rescued from the Epworth fire in 1709 and an account by her of how, as a sixteen year-old, she was terrified by the haunting of the Epworth Rectory. The latter shows she was not without courage because it was she who, at her father's bequest, entered a large, dark garret room and blew a horn in order to hopefully frighten away what they thought was a supernatural intruder. She prayed 'it might have no power over her'. In a poem by her eldest brother she is referred to as 'lusty Anne' – a phrase which then meant someone who was robustly healthy and strong.

Nancy worked for a time as a governess or companion to a family in Thorne, but her sprightly character attracted the attention of a well-educated and well-read local land surveyor called John Lambert. Unlike her sisters, she had found a man that Samuel Wesley was happy to approve. Recognising this was potentially a very good match, her parents scraped together a dowry they could ill afford and, on 2 December 1725, Nancy married Lambert in Holy Trinity Church, Finningley. The following is an extract from a poem written by her brother Samuel to mark the event and it shows just how male-dominated eighteenth-century society was:

> 'Firm let the husband's empire stand,
> with easy but unquestioned sway;
> may he have the kindness to command,
> and thou the bravery to obey!
>
> Long may he give thee comfort, long
> As the frail knot of life shall hold!
> More than a father when thou'rt young,
> More than a son when waxing old.'

Susanna wrote to John Wesley that she hoped 'they will do well' and initially this was the case. Instead of coping with poverty, Nancy found herself not only able to live comfortably but also with enough money to host parties. Her eldest brother Samuel was fearful the new lifestyle might corrupt her but John Wesley assured him this was not the case.

Nancy became almost immediately pregnant and in September 1726 John Wesley became the godfather to her son, who was named John after his father. Most historians have held that this boy died young, but it now argued that he lived long enough to marry and have one child, a girl named Ann after his mother. In 1778 a sea captain called James Jarvis marred an 'Ann Lambert' and the couple emigrated first to New York and then Philadelphia. There is a friendly letter from John Wesley to Mrs Jarvis that is addressed to 'Nancy' and it tells her about the health of his sister Patty (who would, of course, have been Ann's grand-aunt if she was Nancy Wesley's grand-daughter). That is why the American painter John Wesley Jarvis later laid claim to be a descendant of the Wesleys.

Despite having provided Nancy with a dowry they could ill afford, Samuel and Susanna found themselves soon having to offer the couple accommodation because Lambert's wealth suddenly seems to have dissipated because he could not obtain proper employment. Some have surmised this may have been because John Lambert had developed a drink problem. Susanna confided to John Wesley in August 1729:

Hogarth portrays the evils of drink in 'Gin Lane'

'We hear no news of a place for him; though I would fain hope it would please God to provide for him some way ere winter and take off their weight, which really grows very heavy'.

Lambert tried to persuade his brothers-in-law to lend him money (presumably so he could seek to create a new business for himself) but they declined. The assistance provided by Samuel Wesley may explain why Lambert later in gratitude collected his father-in-law's publications, thus preserving what otherwise would in many instances have been lost.

Lambert and Nancy moved to London so he could take up employment there and it is possible Nancy's uncle, Matthew Wesley, helped the couple. Their financial situation significantly improved but Lambert resumed his friendship with his former drinking associate, William Wright, who had married Hetty Wesley. In 1737 Charles Wesley noted with disapproval Wright's bad influence on Lambert and the latter's undesirable liking for spirits. Charles twice recorded how he visited his sister in her home in Hatfield and encouraged Lambert to stop drinking and 'turn again to God'. It was under Charles' influence that John Lambert and Nancy became Methodists. In July 1738 Charles records in his journal preaching to them 'the gospel of forgiveness' and their assent to that.

Rightly or wrongly most historians have assumed Nancy's marriage was happy. Their presence in London so relatively near to the Foundery was a helpful one to the Wesley family. It meant Nancy could be a great source of comfort to her sister Hetty, could tend John when he was taken ill in December 1741, and could help care for her mother Susanna during her final days and be present at her funeral in July 1742. It is interesting that John feared Nancy's more comfortable lifestyle might make her less willing to cope with the people who attended the Foundery and its social outreach to the poor. This was not the case. Far from being offended, she was impressed by the work he was doing and wanted to be part of it. After witnessing him dealing with fifty or sixty people one day, she commented: "I wish I could always be with you. I thought I was in Heaven!"

All this makes it very surprising that a letter from Patty Wesley to John in the autumn of 1746 refers to Nancy having left London to live in Wroot. That presumably would only have happened if something had happened to make living in London no longer possible. Had her husband's business collapsed because of his drinking, forcing the couple to return to Lincolnshire? We simply do not know and, what is worse, there is no further reference to her in any surviving documents, not even when she died.

6. THE LONG-SUFFERING WIFE

The patience of Patty Wesley

Martha (known as 'Patty') Wesley was probably born sometime in the autumn of 1706. After Emily, she was Susanna's favourite, possibly because she was the most 'serious'. There is a story that when all the children except Patty were engaged in noisy fun, their mother entered and reprimanded them, wishing for the day when they would grow up and become more serious. However, when Patty asked if she too would one day become more serious, Susanna laughingly replied that it was not possible for her to become more serious than she already was. Most of her siblings certainly found her a bit too lacking in humour and Charles voiced his and his sisters' feelings when he said it was strange that their mother should so openly have favoured her. As far as he was concerned Patty was a 'grumble-towel' and 'always too wise to be witty'. However, the last charge is not entirely true, even if Patty felt it was. For example, when Charles became a student at Oxford and failed to correspond with her, she wrote to him:

'I once knew a pretty sort of youth in Oxford called Mr Charles Wesley. I should be glad to hear if he is in the land of the living'.

Patty's take on why Susanna favoured her was different:

'What my sisters call partiality was what they might all have enjoyed if they had wished it, which was permission to sit in my mother's chamber when disengaged, to listen to her conversation with others, and to remark on things and books out of school hours'.

Though Charles and his sisters sometimes played pranks on Patty in order to challenge her 'philosophic steadiness', John Wesley never joined in. He shared her more serious approach. Understandably she came to increasingly adore her slightly older brother. Those who knew the family felt she had an almost innate special feeling for John. Adam Clarke, for example, recorded that:

'From the earliest infancy, when a helpless child in the arms [and] afflicted and moaning with pain, the sight of this beloved brother immediately calmed and cheered her, causing her to forget her suffering'.

Interestingly, Patty was facially almost identical to John and it was later said that if she could have dressed like John then people would not have been able to spot any difference between them in terms of their appearance, manners, attitudes, or thoughts. Because it was John who taught her to write, it was commented on that even her handwriting was indistinguishable from his!

When she was about fourteen Patty was sent to stay for a time with her uncle, Matthew Wesley, in London. His household was far less overtly religious than she was used to, but it gave her the opportunity to visit her eldest brother Samuel at Westminster and to attend worship at St Paul's Cathedral and St Dunstan's Church in Fleet Street. By the time Patty returned home to Epworth in 1723 she had grown into a very attractive young woman. That Christmas her father visited his friends, the Granthams, who lived in Kelstern. Unbeknown to Patty, he won their assent to her becoming a governess to their children. Meanwhile Patty, like her sister Hetty, was attracted to John Romley who was acting as her father's curate. He was equally attracted to her, but, unfortunately for Patty, their ability to see each other came to an abrupt end when her father overheard Romley singing a song that he deemed vulgar. He dismissed him and banned him from the house.

John Wesley, whom Patty closely resembled

Shortly afterwards, Patty was told of the agreement that had been made for her to go to the Grantham family and her father refused to listen to her pleas not to be sent away. From Kelstern Patty sent a letter in March 1725 to her brother John and voiced her anguish at being separated from Romley:

'You know that my father forbade him his house … since which time I have never seen Romley. He wrote me several times since, and we held a secret correspondence together for a little time before I came to Kelstern. I desire you would not be so inquisitive how the intrigue broke off; the bare mention of it is much, much more than I can bear…. I came [here] very much against my consent, and had far rather have gone to my grave!… I am in no great measure careless what becomes of me. Home I would not go to, were I reduced to beggary, and here I will never stay, where they tell me that they should never have desired my company only my father proffered me, and they did not know well how to refuse me.'

She told John she hoped at some stage to seek her fortune in London and that she was resolved not to marry until either she had learned to forget Romley or else have her relationship with him accepted. Her burden was made worse by her loneliness: 'I have no company but my fellow servants….[and] I am condemned to constant solitude'.

Some historians have argued Samuel was right in preventing either Hetty or Patty becoming involved with Romley. However, that is based largely on the fact in later years he refused to let John Wesley preach at Epworth and developed a drink problem. In fact there are reasons to explain both of these things without assuming Romley was a bad man. First, one can easily argue that his rejection of John was a natural reaction from a man who had been slighted by the family. Secondly, his drink problem appears to have arisen because he developed a throat affliction and his parishioners, who liked him, plied him with liquor in the mistaken belief this would provide a cure.

Patty's hopes of somehow escaping to London were just wishful thinking, but in the summer of 1725 she was permitted to return home, either because the Granthams had made all too clear they did not want her any more or because the family crisis over Hetty's behaviour made Samuel reluctant to permit Patty to be out of his sight. In September she wrote to John, describing her life as 'ruined':

'I believe there will never be any provision made for me, but when my father dies I shall have my choice of three things, starving, going to a common service, or marrying meanly as my sisters have done'.

From her perspective Sukey had acquired a terrible husband, Nancy was about to marry a man who lacked religious faith, and Hetty was being made to marry a good-natured but unsuitable man.

Given her confidences to John, Patty was hurt by his failure to find time in Oxford to write to her. In February 1727 she expressed her pain that he was writing to her sisters Emily and Nancy rather than her:

'Though I cannot possibly be so vain as to think that I do for my own personal merits deserve more love than my sisters, yet can you blame me if I sometimes wish I had been so happy as to have had the first place in your heart?'

By then she was feeling even more isolated because there were plans for Emily and Kezzy to go to Lincoln. In effect, except for her crippled sister Molly, Patty would then be the only daughter forced to stay with her parents. That summer she was brought low by a fever.

When she recovered she was sent to London. It is not clear exactly when this happened but it may have been as late as 1729. The reason for permitting this to happen was almost certainly that her uncle Matthew Wesley had become ill and required nursing. Matthew Wesley's wealth meant Patty for the first time in years wanted for 'neither money nor clothes'. Her brother Samuel's wife accused her of giving herself 'airs' but this was probably simple jealousy rather than truly reflective of any change in Patty's behaviour. Once Matthew had recovered, he took Patty back to Epworth in 1731. However, he was deeply shocked by the poverty he found there. As a consequence he asked if Patty could return back to London with him, promising in effect to adopt her and see to her future. This was agreed and he and Patty returned, visiting en route her sisters Emily and Kezzy in Lincoln.

Back in London, the question of whom Patty should marry was uppermost in the family's thinking. John recommended she should remain celibate but there is no doubt that she felt any marriage would be better than none: 'I may as well be contented with one I am not very fond of now as stay till I am destitute'. She was courted by a man called Johnson, but turned him down because he seemed to lack the prospect of becoming sufficiently wealthy to suit her needs. Her brother John recommended she marry a young graduate from Lincoln College called Matthew Horbery but Patty said, though he was a good conversationalist, he was no more a lover than 'a Grand Turk'. For a while she spent time with Benjamin Ingham, another of her brother's contacts, but this came to nothing. It was eventually a deeply pious and handsome clergyman called Westley Hall who finally won her acceptance. This may have been because of his natural charm but the fact he was a particular protégé of her adored brother probably helped.

Westley had told John he knew God wanted him to remain celibate so John did not put him forward as a possible husband, but Patty knew John thought him 'a pattern of lowliness, meekness, seriousness.... and above all of self-denial'. In 1734 the couple agreed that they would marry but Westley made Patty vow to keep this a secret. Shortly afterwards he went to Epworth with John and there he met the vivacious Kezzy Wesley. Forgetting Patty, he began to court her younger sister and Kezzy, unaware of the situation, responded. He informed John, who knew nothing of his relationship with Patty, that he had heard God's voice telling him to abandon celibacy and to marry Kezzy. According to John:

'He took all the freedom with her that was consistent with modesty, and such as I thought her reserved temper would have never allowed to any but an actual husband. My father and mother soon observed it... He could not now bear an hour's separation, insomuch that all the servants, as well as occasional visitants that we had, began to ask 'When Miss Kezzy was to be married?'.... [He told] my sister that he would be hers, only hers, for ever'.

However, when Westley returned to London he had second thoughts about what he had said to Kezzy. This probably stemmed from the fact he received letters from her brother-in-law John Whitelamb blackening her reputation, even though John Wesley told him to ignore the false allegations. Westley secretly resumed his relationship with Patty, who was unaware of what had happened in Lincolnshire. This may have gone unnoticed because the dominant issue among the Wesleys at this time was the imminent death of their father Samuel. Patty visited him in the early spring of 1735. Whilst she was there, John and Charles also arrived and Westley accompanied them. Unbelievable though it sounds, somehow he managed to keep both Patty and Kezzy unaware of the extent to which he had committed himself to both of them. Kezzy appears to have recognized that he had been making advances to Patty, but he gave her reassurances that he now loved her.

Samuel Wesley died on 25 April 1735. With Patty back in London, Westley's intentions reverted back to her, possibly in response to further attacks on Kezzy's character from the pen of Whitelamb. This may explain why in June Kezzy wrote a letter to her brother John saying she now thought her future lay in celibacy rather than marriage. What was happening probably went unnoticed that summer by both John and Charles Wesley because they were involved in the process of making arrangements to become missionaries to America. Westley was invited to join them but he eventually declined, partly because Patty opposed him going and partly because his mother managed to obtain a curacy for him at Wootton Rivers in Gloucestershire. He told John Wesley he wished to stay because he had received 'a counter-revelation' from God to marry Patty and not Kezzy and he asked John to marry them before he left for America.

John was amazed by this unexpected jilting of Kezzy and refused to marry them. He tried to persuade Patty to drop Hall, saying 'she could not marry with innocence' given his relationship with her sister. When Patty stood by her decision, John made clear Westley could never marry her without first obtaining the approval of their mother and uncle. To his dismay Westley quickly obtained not only the backing of Matthew Wesley but also the promise of a £500 dowry. Matthew, of course, knew nothing of the promises that had been made to Kezzy. It is not clear exactly what Patty told her mother but Susanna also consented, presumably glad to have another daughter married now that she was reduced to being a homeless widow. With the marriage agreed, Westley appears to have visited Kezzy, presumably to break the news. However, obviously his intentions did not hold because when they met he instead proffered her a friendship ring, saying it was a token of his love until he could offer her a marriage ring! This did not prevent him a few days later marrying Patty on 13 September 1735.

The wedding was extolled in verse in the 'Gentleman's Magazine':

> 'Hymen, light thy purest flame,
> Every sacred rite prepare,
> Never to thy altar came
> A more pious, faithful pair'.

However, none of Patty's three brothers agreed with these sentiments because they believed Hall should have married Kezzy. When Kezzy was taken ill, Charles attributed this to her having had her heart broken and wrote a scathing attack on Patty's behaviour:

> 'Sooner shall light in league with darkness join,
> Virtue and Vice, and heaven and hell, combine,
> Than her pure soul consent to mix with thine;
> To share thy sin, adopt thy perjury,
> And damn herself to be revenged on thee;
> To load her conscience with a sister's blood,
> The guilt of incest, and the curse of God!'

Patty had to reveal to them the whole truth of her prior engagement. Quite understandably this cleared her but presented Westley in a very bad light. Her three brothers all voiced their unhappiness. Samuel said:

'Brother Hall's is a black story.... His tongue is too smoothe for my roughness, and rather inclines me to suspect than believe [him].'

John agreed Hall had been duplicitous, and Charles summed up his and his brothers' feelings by saying Patty 'should not have mismatched herself with so worthless a man'.

The marriage controversy was overshadowed by the fact both John and Charles were in the final stages of their preparations for travelling as missionaries to the American colony of Georgia. They boarded their ship on 14 October. By then it had been agreed that Samuel would look after their mother Susanna but there was no agreement over what should happen to Kezzy. Samuel had offered to also look after her, but only if John Wesley contributed money towards her upkeep. John had declined to do so. In this situation Kezzy agreed to go and live with Patty and Westley. Samuel was so disgusted he cut off all communications with her. However, her mother Susanna eventually decided to leave Samuel and also go to Wootton Rivers. In August 1737 she wrote:

'Mr Hall and his wife are very good to me. He behaves like a gentleman and a Christian, and my daughter with as much duty and tenderness as can be expected; so that on this account I am very easy'.

Patty needed her mother and sister because she was regularly pregnant and each time her infant child died. In December 1737 Westley gained a better church at Fisherton, a village near Salisbury and both Susanna and Kezzy followed him and Patty there. Only when John Wesley returned from America in 1738 were arrangements made for Kezzy to go elsewhere. Westley became a supporter of the early Methodist movement and this meant he and Patty regularly visited London between 1739 and 1741. Susanna ceased to live with them and, alongside her eldest daughter Emilia, moved into the Foundery, the centre of John and Charles' work. That Westley's immoral behaviour before marrying Patty was forgotten is evidenced by the fact that, when Susanna died in 1742, John looked to the Halls to replace her as the stabilizing presence among the society members at the Foundery.

However, Westley declined John's offer because he had decided to work independently in Salisbury. He announced he was leaving the Anglican Church in order to set up a dissenting society. John thought this decision stemmed from the fact Westley had allowed himself to fall under the influence of the Moravians who had 'infused into him as much as they could of their contempt of me and my brother'. In a letter to Patty he expressed his hope that Westley would regain his former regard for them. However, the same letter showed a cruelly insensitive approach to the family having just lost yet another infant child:

'I believe the death of your children is a great instance of the goodness of God towards you. You have often mentioned how much of your time they took up. Now that time is restored to you, and you have nothing to do but to serve the Lord…. without distraction'.

Patty had a total of ten children in the course of her marriage but nine died in infancy. Nevertheless, such tragedies seemed to strengthen rather than diminish her faith. Typical is this account of how her sense of God's presence was strengthened in 1743:

'I was one evening retired into my chamber, with a design to spend some time in private prayer; but before I kneeled down, all at once…. I had a clear sense that the Lamb of God had made an atonement for me; that he had made full satisfaction for my sins….. Hallelujah!'

Salisbury where Westley Hall became a minister

In that same year Westley accused John of allowing himself to be 'led captive in the bonds of uncharitableness' towards him. John's response was unequivocal:

'You are a weak, injudicious, fickle, irresolute man, deeply enthusiastic, and highly opiniated of yourself…. [You] jilted one of my sisters and married the other…. Your life has been one blunder ever since'.

Not surprisingly Westley responded by cutting all links with the Wesleys. It says much for Patty's courage that she expressed her continued loyalty to her brothers and refused to leave the Church. Her brother Charles wrote in August 1743:

'I got with my sister Hall in Salisbury. She stands alone. Every soul of her husband's society has forsaken the ordinances of God; for which reason she refuses to belong to it'.

Two years later he expressed his admiration that Patty was still refusing to leave the Church despite being 'mocked and persecuted' and he described her as 'a rock in the midst of waves'.

All this did little to help the relations between Patty and her husband. This may have been a factor in why Westley began turning to other women. He seduced a young seamstress and then made sure he was away in London when she went into labour. It was the servants who had to tell the unsuspecting Patty that her husband was responsible. It says much for her character that she insisted on the girl being properly cared for before going to London to confront Westley with his actions. When Charles Wesley told Patty he could not understand how she could bring herself to aid her husband's concubine, she made a reply that truly reveals her kind nature. She said that she knew many would regard it as 'meritorius to abandon her to the distress which she has brought upon herself' but she had to help 'the poor hapless creature' because 'I did not act as a woman but as a Christian'.

The clearest picture of Westley's sexual misbehaviour comes from an account written by John Wesley in 1747:

'He began very frequently to kiss the women of the society, and sometimes to take them in his arms, telling them this was Christian fellowship, and a part of the communion of saints. This 'spiritual love', as he termed it, he constantly showed to several of the women leaders'.

This soon led him to 'take unusual freedoms' with a young woman called Elizabeth Greenway. She resisted but he then took 'greater freedoms than before, not at all consistent with modesty', saying 'he looked upon her as a wife'. Elizabeth eventually succumbed so Westley 'frequently committed everything with her which could be done without her being with child'. This led him to then seek to add other women to his conquests. Some resisted, such as Jane Moody, who 'violently broke loose and ran away'. Others surrendered, such as Mary Merrifield, who announced 'God had revealed to her that she was his wife and was to bear him three children'.

Poor Patty found herself in an appalling situation. Sometimes Westley would leave home for months and sometimes he would throw her out of her home (on these occasions she usually took temporary refuge in the Foundery). In December 1747 she confided in John that she felt as if she was living under a catastrophic storm and 'I sometimes doubt whether I must ever be delivered in this world or no'. It was also not long before he was making Patty look after his illegitimate offspring. To make things even more difficult for a woman of her faith, Westley acquired increasingly odd religious beliefs to justify his behaviour. His opposition to Patty's brothers' evangelical work also increased. In 1750, for example, Patty sought temporary refuge in Bristol but Westley followed her, forced his way into the chapel and dragged her away in front of her brother Charles' horrified eyes.

Publicly Patty remained loyal to her husband but privately many years later she confided to Charles' daughter Sally:

'The seeds of all his profligacy were deeply rooted in him, and they would have produced their corresponding fruits had he been married to an angel. He was a man of no mind, and but little judgment; acting, not by rule or reason, but by impulse; and fickleness and imbecility are the mildest terms which can be applied to his singular compound character of piety and profligacy'.

There were at least two occasions when Patty seriously thought of leaving him. She asked him to give her a small allowance so they could live apart because it was obvious 'I cannot possibly oblige you any longer by anything I say or do'. However, she felt her wedding vow made separation wrong. No woman should dispute the authority God had given husband over wife. In one letter to Westley she wrote:

'You may remember whenever I was angry enough to talk of leaving you, you could never work me up to such a height as to make me say I would never return'.

Throughout her continued problems Patty felt buoyed up by God. She wrote in her journal in 1752:

'Infinite still is thy mercy towards thy unworthy servant, else I should sink all at once; no longer could I possibly bear up under such a weight of sorrow'.

And in 1756 she reflected that it was always important to reflect on one's own sinfulness when coping with the sins of others:

'O may I never entertain one thought of any neglect I have met with from a fellow-worm without deeply considering how far more guilty I am myself'.

Having embraced polygamy, Westley saw no reason to cease having sexual relations with Patty whenever he chose. Their only child to survive infancy was a boy whom she named 'Wesley'. The only recorded instance of Patty seriously challenging her husband's domestic authority was when he locked Wesley inside a dark closet as a punishment for a fairly trivial offence and refused to let him out, even when the child was screaming in terror. She told Westley she would refuse to look after the illegitimate child she was at that time caring for if he did not immediately release her son. Sadly Wesley Hall died from smallpox at the age of fourteen whilst attending a boarding school (John and Charles had agreed to pay fees to ensure his good education). Though deeply distressed, Patty never complained, judging it to be the will of God.

Charles Wesley tried to comfort her by writing two hymns about her loss and these were included in a book entitled 'Funeral Hymns' in 1769. They spoke of the pain of seeing 'the blooming youth that charmed our eyes.... cut down and withered in an hour' but the hope that he was now with God:

> 'Rest, happy saint! With God secure,
> Lodged in the bosom of the Lamb;
> Thy joy is full, thy state is sure;
> Through all eternity the same;
> The heavenly doors have shut thee in...'

Eventually sometime in the mid-1750s Westley permanently deserted Patty, taking with him one of his 'wives' and going to work first in Ireland and then in the West Indies. Despite this, John Wesley did not have much time for his deserted sister. In 1761, for example, he commented that it was 'strange that so few of my relations should be of any use to me in the work of God' and bemoaned that she and Emily had 'kept at a distance' and 'never heartily joined in the work'. He attributed this to them lacking 'resolution, spirit, [and] patience'.

It is said that years later Westley returned to Patty 'professing penitential sorrow' and she took him in and nursed him till his death in December 1775. He told those around his deathbed: 'I have injured an angel! an angel that never reproached me'. Some historians question whether this actually happened but it is certain that Westley repented because John Wesley wrote in his journal on 2 January 1776:

'I came just time enough, not to see, but to bury poor Mr Hall, my brother-in-law, who died on Wednesday morning; I trust in peace, for God had given him deep repentance. Such another monument of divine mercy, considering how low he had fallen'.

Released from her turbulent life with her husband, Patty lived with her sister Emily until Emily died in 1771. Patty's intelligence and kindness won her many admirers. She became increasingly friendly with Dr Samuel Johnson, who was the most distinguished literary figure in London. He rated her conversation very highly and often invited her to his house so they could discuss theological and moral issues and engage in literary debates. Her favourite theme was the goodness of God. It is said that on one occasion when Johnson was bemoaning the unhappiness of human life, Patty told him that was because he had 'always lived among the wits, not the saints' and that those who knew God had 'true happiness'. In February 1784 she introduced him to her brother John but Dr Johnson was not impressed, mainly one suspects because John always made clear that there were more important things to do than talk with him. Dr Johnson told his friend Boswell that John's conversation was enchanting but 'he is never at leisure … [and] is always obliged to go at a certain hour'.

Patty with Dr Johnson and her brother John

By all accounts Patty was a woman whose faith was a constant source of inner peace. She said on one occasion: 'Evil was not kept from me; but evil has been kept from harming me'. Her faith also found expression in constant acts of kindness. Charles Wesley said there was no use giving any money to improve the conditions under which Patty lived because she would immediately give the money to someone poorer than herself. It was noticed that, though she would staunchly oppose anything sinful, she never tried to condemn the sinner:

'Few persons could be mentioned of whom she had not something good to say; and if their faults were glaring, she would plead the influence of circumstances, education, and sudden temptation… Her manner of reproving sin was so gentle, so evidently the effect of love, that no one was ever known to be offended at it. Young people were so certain of her kindness, if they erred, that she was often chosen as a confessor among them'.

In old age Patty drew very close to her niece Sally, especially after first Charles and then John died. Sally was amazed at her aunt's serenity, given her troubled life. It is said that Sally grew increasingly concerned that her aged aunt still insisted on taking long walks, even though her slow steps posed a hazard when crossing roads. On one occasion Sally had to pull her out of the way of a carriage and this resulted in Patty falling to the ground. She then calmly told her niece that in future she must recognize falling was a greater risk than being run over because coachmen would do all they could to avoid getting involved in an accident. She was in fact amazingly fit for her age and in 1788 John Wesley was still able to refer to Patty as being 'a very young old woman'.

It was old age rather than a specific illness that eventually led to her death. What little she possessed she bequeathed to Sally, who asked permission to be with her when she lay dying. Patty told her she could stay 'but I charge you not to grieve for me more than half an hour'. Sally said it was a triumph of faith that a woman so 'weighed down with weaknesses and infirmities' should show such calmness and composure. The last survivor of the Epworth family died at the age of eighty-five on 12 July 1791. Her last words to Sally were: 'I have the assurance [of salvation] which I have long prayed for. Shout!' Sally later wrote:

'She spoke no more, and the happy spirit passed so easily we could not ascertain the moment of its flight'.

It was agreed that Patty should be buried in the same vault with the remains of John, who had died shortly before her. On her tomb were inscribed a text from Proverbs: 'She opened her mouth with wisdom, and in her tongue was the law of kindness'. There is no doubt that the early writers about Methodism picked up a picture of her as being virtually a saint from those who had known her:

'She had a soul so magnanimous, so devoid of self, so unmoved by injury, so steadily religious, so compassionate to her fellow creatures, so thoroughly devoted to God, that her equal will rarely be found among women'.

❑ ❑ ❑ ❑ ❑

7. UNFULFILLED PROMISE

The story of Kezzy Wesley, the one daughter to escape marriage

Kezia or Kezzy Wesley was born in March 1709, the last of the children of Samuel and Susanna Wesley. Little is known about her childhood other than as a six-year old she entered into a foot-stamping competition with the alleged ghost that briefly haunted the Rectory. It is sometimes implied that her education may have been given less attention than her older sisters either because Susanna's attention was more taken up with the education of John and Charles or because Kezzy showed less aptitude. This is based on a comment by Susanna that Kezzy was 'more years learning than any of the rest had been in months'. In fact, if Kezzy was not as highly educated as some of her sisters, that may simply be because she appears to have suffered from frequent ill health. Moreover, she was still better educated than most girls and that explains why her sister Emily was able to have her appointed as an assistant at the school belonging to Mrs. Taylor in Lincoln in 1727.

From a letter written by Kezzy in January 1729 it would appear her brother John had encouraged her to marry a man of his choice rather than struggle in a post that only offered her board and kept her deprived of money and clothes. In her reply Kezzy says she has no desire to be a burden on any of her relations, but she had no intention of marrying. She says the man 'might be worthy of love' but she cannot see his good qualities and would prefer to 'live the life of a nun'. She also criticizes John for describing her as being pretty, saying she was very happy to receive his guidance on how she should live her life but not to receive compliments about 'having a beautiful face or a fine shape':

'Perhaps you might think it would please the vanity of our sex to be flattered. Know then, I am not yet vain enough to be pleased with flattery'.

In a letter in July Kezzy recounted the privations facing her and the family, making reference not only to her own long-standing health problems, but the declining health of her mother 'occasioned by her want of clothes or convenient meat' and her sister Sukey because of her unhappy marriage. She reiterated her intention not to burden the family by returning home and to continue working in Lincoln, despite her unhappy position. Bemoaning her lack of 'faith and patience', she asked John to excuse all her faults. There is in Kezzy's writings a clear theme of her feeling inferior to the rest of the family. In one letter she writes:

'I could not have imagined that it would be any pleasure to a person of sense to hear from such an illiterate person, had I not had it from your own hand and seal'.

Forced to return home in 1730 by Mrs. Taylor's failure to pay her for her work, Kezzy found life difficult, not least because her health was very poor. She hated in particular having to witness the unhappy marriage of her sister Sukey. In 1731 she was back in Lincoln trying to earn her living again. She told John:

'Here I have time…. [but no books to read]. At home I had books, but no time, because constant illness made me incapable of study'.

She sought his advice how she should best occupy her time in improving her education but did not find it helpful when he recommended books she could neither borrow nor afford to buy. She found it even harder to bear her position when her sister Patty had the good fortune to be invited to stay with their uncle in London, whilst she was forced once again to return home. It would appear that she began taking snuff, possibly in the vain hope it would ease her depressed state.

As we have seen in a previous chapter, Kezzy was caught up in the storm over Whitelamb's betrayal of her sister Molly and he never forgave her opposition to their marriage. He did his utmost to denigrate her character, especially after Molly's death in 1734. By then Kezzy was the only daughter still left in Epworth. It was in this situation that she was swept off her feet by Westley Hall, only to eventually find out that he had prior promised himself to her sister Patty, whom he subsequently married in 1735. Kezzy philosophically told her brother John:

'I think a single life is the more excellent way; and there are several reasons why I rather desire to continue as I am…. [though] my relations are continually soliciting me to marry'.

Charles Wesley and John Gambold

Interestingly, the chief reason she gives for avoiding marriage is 'the great duty a wife owes a husband'. Given the way some of her sisters were being treated by their husbands, it is hardly surprising that Kezzy felt she did not want to be in their position.

Unfortunately when Samuel Wesley died in 1735, she found herself – like her mother – suddenly homeless. Susanna initially went to stay with her daughter Emily, leaving Kezzy with the prospect of going alone to her eldest brother's home in Tiverton. Kezzy felt her mother had abandoned her as being 'a weak, entangled, wretched thing'. To the surprise of her family, she opted not to stay in the home of Samuel and instead to live with Patty, even though that meant also living with Westley Hall who had treated her so badly. She may have decided on this because it was obvious her brother Samuel's wife was not happy about housing her unless John Wesley contributed to her upkeep – and John was not prepared to do that. In a later letter Kezzy refers to how much her mind and body at this time was weakened by 'ill-usage' and how she could not bear 'any roughness without either being angry or rejected'.

Her living with the Halls did not meet with the approval of any of her brothers, especially Charles who said he was shocked beyond measure. After Charles' return from America, arrangements were made for her to stay with the family of one of his friends, the Rev. Henry Piers, Vicar of Bexley. It was perhaps for that reason that a budding relationship with 'a gentleman' in Salisbury came to nothing. Nevertheless, Kezzy soon established a happy relationship with not only the Piers family but also the Rev John Gambold, who had been one of her brothers' associates in Oxford. She began paying regular visits to his family home at Stanton Harcourt and for the first time in her adult life she was truly happy. Charles visited her whenever he could and the two became very close. She looked to him to become her spiritual mentor. He wrote in September 1737:

'She fell upon my neck, and in a flood of tears, begged me to pray for her…. She was full of earnest wishes for divine love; owned there was a depth in religion she had never fathomed; that she was not, but longed to be, converted; would give up all to obtain the love of God….. I prayed over her, and blessed God from my heart…. [She] was convinced that all her misery proceeded from her not loving God'.

It was Kezzy who acted as Charles' nurse when he was taken seriously ill with pleurisy in March 1738 – indeed, without her care he may well not have survived. She spent so much time looking after him that her own health collapsed. When Charles experienced assurance of his salvation in May 1738, he immediately wanted Kezzy and Hetty to have the same happen to them. The two sisters proved initially hostile to his new-found evangelical faith because they could not see why Charles felt he had not been a true Christian before. This led him to threaten he would cease seeing Kezzy and she immediately broke down in tears. Over the next couple of years she grew ever closer to his way of thinking – as indeed did Hetty as well.

According to Patty, Kezzy began to form a relationship with another man, but, if so, this was affected by her increasingly frail health. She died on 9 March 1741, aged only thirty-two. Charles, who comforted her in her final hours, wrote:

'Full of thankfulness, resignation and love, without pain or trouble, she commended her spirit into the hands of Jesus, and fell asleep.'

There is no doubt that John Wesley attributed Kezzy's death to what had happened earlier with Westley Hall. He accused him of having 'stolen Kezia from the God of her youth', saying from then on she had 'refused to be comforted and fell into a lingering illness'. Most historians have not accepted John's verdict but the ill-fated affair certainly did not help Kezzy's state of mind, reinforcing as it did her sense of inferiority and unworthiness. Whatever promise her life had once held, it was never fulfilled.

❑ ❑ ❑ ❑ ❑